Qatar Travel Guide

2023

A Comprehensive Travel Handbook

Fodor Elise

Table Of Contents

Chapter One

Introduction

Qatar's lifestyle can differ greatly depending on the area and personal choices, but there are some commonalities that give a general idea of what to expect.

Many begin their day with a relaxed breakfast at home, which typically includes bread, butter, jam and coffee. Then, they proceed to work or school, where the workday starts at 8:00 am and ends at 6:00 pm, with lunch at noon.
Lunch is usually a relaxed meal, which can include dishes like Majboos, Luqaimat, and Kousa mahshi.

In the evenings, people engage in various activities like going to the gym, pursuing hobbies or clubs, or spending time with loved ones.

Dinner is usually served later in the evening, around 7:00 pm or 8:00 pm, and it's usually a more substantial meal than lunch.
In Qatar, the evening routine is similar to that of Western countries, with many engaging in activities such as watching television, reading, or other forms of leisure before bedtime.

However, lifestyle can vary greatly depending on the location, with rural areas tending to have a more traditional focus on agriculture and a slower pace of life, while urban areas may have a faster pace and greater emphasis on work and leisure activities.

In general, Qataris prioritize good food, cultural pursuits, and a balanced work-life. Additionally, they place a strong importance on maintaining personal relationships and social connections, often spending time with friends and family regularly.

Qatar is a small country located in the Middle East, on the northeastern coast of the Arabian Peninsula. It is bordered by Saudi Arabia to the south and the Persian Gulf to the north and east. Qatar is an absolute monarchy, with the Emir of Qatar as the head of state and government. The official language is Arabic and the currency is the Qatari Riyal.

Qatar has the world's third-largest natural gas reserves and is the world's largest exporter of liquified natural gas. The country's economy is heavily dependent on its oil and gas industries, but it has also made efforts to diversify its economy in recent years. Qatar is known for its modern architecture, including the iconic Aspire Tower, and for hosting the 2022 FIFA World Cup.

Qatar has a population of around 2.8 million people, of which only around 10-15% are Qatari citizens. The rest are mostly expatriate workers from other countries in the Middle East, South Asia, and Southeast Asia.

The country has a high standard of living and a diverse culture, with influences from both traditional Bedouin and modern Western cultures.

Qatar has a rapidly developing infrastructure, with many new highways, airports, and skyscrapers being built in recent years. The country is also known for its museums, such as the Museum of Islamic Art and the National Museum of Qatar, and for its shopping destinations, including the Villaggio Mall and the souqs in the capital city of Doha.

Qatar is also home to several prestigious educational institutions, including Qatar University, the Weill Cornell Medical College, and the Texas A&M University at Qatar.

In terms of tourism, Qatar has been focusing on developing its tourism industry in recent years, with the goal of attracting more visitors to the country. Qatar is known for its luxury resorts, beaches, and desert landscapes, as well as its rich history and culture.

In 2022 Qatar will host the FIFA World Cup, which is expected to bring a significant number of tourists to the country and further boost its economy.

Chapter Two

Geography And Climate Of Qatar

Qatar is a small country located in the Middle East, on the northeastern coast of the Arabian Peninsula. It is bordered by Saudi Arabia to the south and the Persian Gulf to the north and east. The capital of Qatar is Doha.

Geographically, Qatar is mostly desert with flat terrain. The majority of the country is covered by sand dunes, while the remaining area is composed of rocky and gravel plains. The highest point in Qatar is Qurayn Abu al Bawl at 103 meters (338 ft).

Qatar is also home to many wadis, or dry riverbeds, which are filled with water only during heavy rainfalls.

Qatar has a hot desert climate, with high temperatures and low rainfall. The temperature in Qatar can reach up to 50 degrees Celsius (122 degrees Fahrenheit) during the summer months. Winter temperatures are more mild, with an average of around 25 degrees Celsius (77 degrees Fahrenheit). Rainfall is rare in Qatar, with an annual average of only around 100 millimeters (4 inches). Most of the rainfall occurs in the winter months.

The lack of rainfall in Qatar makes it one of the driest places on earth.

However, the country has managed to sustain a population and support agriculture through a combination of desalination, underground water sources, and irrigation. Qatar also has a large oil and natural gas industry, which has made it one of the wealthiest countries in the world.

In conclusion, Qatar is a small country located in the Middle East, characterized by its hot desert climate and lack of rainfall. Despite the harsh environmental conditions, Qatar has managed to sustain a population and support agriculture and industry through the use of technology and resources.

In addition to its hot desert climate and lack of rainfall, Qatar also experiences high humidity levels, particularly during the summer months. This can make the heat feel even more oppressive. The country also occasionally experiences dust storms, which can reduce visibility and make it difficult for residents to go about their daily activities.

Despite the harsh climate, Qatar has a diverse and unique ecosystem. The country is home to a variety of desert animals, such as the Arabian oryx, the desert hare, and the sand gazelle. Birds such as the desert lark, the desert finch, and the houbara bustard can also be found in Qatar.

The country also has a number of protected areas, including the Al-Shahaniya Reserve and the Al-Zubara Fort and Archaeological Area, which offer visitors the opportunity to explore and learn about Qatar's natural and cultural heritage.

Qatar's economy is heavily dependent on its oil and natural gas reserves, which account for a significant portion of the country's GDP. Additionally, Qatar has been investing in other industries, such as tourism and real estate, in order to diversify its economy. The country is also home to many international companies and organizations, including the Qatar Foundation and the Qatar Science & Technology Park.

Qatar's population is made up of a diverse mix of people from various nationalities, with a significant number of expatriates. The country has a high standard of living and offers a wide range of employment opportunities, particularly in the oil and gas, construction, and service sectors. Qatar also offers modern infrastructure and a tax-free income for expatriates, which makes it a popular destination for professionals and businesses. Despite this, there have been criticisms of the country's treatment of migrant workers, as well as concerns about the country's human rights record.

Chapter Three

History And Culture You Will Find In Qatar

Qatar has a rich history and culture that dates back to the Neolithic period. The Qatar Peninsula has been inhabited for thousands of years by various tribes, including the Al-Maadeed, Al-Zubara, and Al-Jumali.

The Qatar Peninsula was also a key location for trade and commerce in ancient times, with links to Mesopotamia, India, and China. Qatar's pearl industry was particularly important during the 19th and early 20th centuries.

Qatar has traditionally been a Bedouin society, with a strong sense of community and tribal identity. The Bedouin way of life is reflected in the country's customs and traditions, such as the weekly souq (market) and the annual camel race.

Islam is the dominant religion in Qatar, and the country's Islamic heritage is reflected in its architecture, such as the beautiful Mosques and Islamic art and calligraphy. The country's Islamic heritage is also evident in its festivals, such as Eid al-Fitr and Eid al-Adha.

Qatar is also home to a diverse and multicultural population, including many expatriates from around the world.

This diversity is reflected in the country's cuisine, which includes a wide variety of international dishes as well as traditional Qatari dishes such as machboos and harees. The country has undergone significant development in recent years, with the construction of modern skyscrapers and infrastructure, but still, the country's traditional heritage is well-preserved and celebrated through various festivals and events.

In addition to its rich history and culture, Qatar is also known for its strong emphasis on education and the arts. Qatar Foundation, established by the country's former Emir, Sheikh Hamad bin Khalifa Al Thani, has played a major role in promoting education and cultural awareness in the country. Qatar Foundation has established several educational institutions, including Qatar Academy, which offers an American-style education, and the Qatar Faculty of Islamic Studies, which is dedicated to the study of Islamic civilization.

The country also has several museums and cultural institutions that showcase its history and heritage, such as the Museum of Islamic Art, which houses a collection of Islamic art and artifacts from around the world, and the Qatar National Museum, which tells the story of the country's history and culture.

In recent years, Qatar has also become known for its efforts to promote and support contemporary art and culture.

The country is home to several major museums and institutions, such as the Museum of Modern Art and the Mathaf: Arab Museum of Modern Art, which showcase the works of local and international artists.

In addition, Qatar also hosts several festivals and events throughout the year to celebrate its culture and heritage, such as the Qatar International Food Festival, which features a variety of international and local cuisine, and the Qatar National Day, which marks the country's independence from the British protectorate.

Overall, Qatar has a rich and diverse history and culture that reflects its Bedouin heritage, Islamic traditions, and its role as a major center of trade and commerce in the region. The country has made great efforts to preserve and celebrate its heritage, while also embracing and promoting contemporary art and culture.

Chapter Four

Mode Of Transportation In Qatar

Qatar has a well-developed transportation infrastructure, which includes both public and private options. The primary mode of transportation in Qatar is by car, as the country has a high ownership rate of vehicles. The public transportation system in Qatar is relatively limited, but it is undergoing expansion and modernization. The Doha Metro, which is currently under construction, is expected to greatly improve the public transportation options in the country. Additionally, there are also buses and taxis available for public use.

Qatar also has a well-developed road network, including several expressways, making it easy to travel by car. Furthermore, Qatar has an international airport and a seaport, providing options for air and sea travel.

In addition to the modes of transportation mentioned earlier, Qatar also has a number of options for those who prefer active or sustainable transportation. For example, there are bike lanes and paths throughout the country, as well as bike-sharing programs.

Qatar also has a number of parks and nature reserves where people can go for a walk or bike ride. Furthermore, Qatar has a number of pedestrian walkways and bridges, making it easy to navigate the city on foot.

Qatar's transportation infrastructure is constantly evolving, and the government is investing heavily in transportation projects to improve the country's mobility and connectivity. The government has also implemented several policies and initiatives to encourage the use of sustainable transportation options and reduce traffic congestion.

Overall, Qatar offers a variety of transportation options, including public and private options, active and sustainable options, and options for both short and long-distance travel. The government is actively working to improve the transportation infrastructure and make it more efficient, safe and sustainable.

Chapter Five

Accommodation In Qatar

Qatar offers a variety of accommodation options, including luxury hotels, serviced apartments, and budget-friendly options. Luxury hotels are prevalent in the capital city of Doha, with many international hotel chains represented. These hotels typically offer high-end amenities such as spas, swimming pools, and fine dining restaurants. Serviced apartments, which offer more space and flexibility than traditional hotel rooms, are also a popular option in Qatar.

For those on a budget, there are also budget hotels and hostels available.

Additionally, there are also many vacation rental options available, including villas and apartments for short-term rent.

I recall the initial occasion when I secured lodging in one of the most picturesque cities in Qatar.

I had longed to visit the metropolis, known for its picturesque architecture, abundant history, and lively cultural atmosphere.

When I finally had the opportunity to go, I was determined to find the ideal spot to stay. After investigating online, I chose to book a small guesthouse situated in the center of the city.

The guesthouse was housed in a lovely, historic building and provided a variety of amenities such as a private bathroom, a comfortable bed, and a kitchenette.

When I arrived, I was impressed by the guesthouse's charm and atmosphere. The room was decorated in a traditional Qatar style with antique furniture and original artwork on the walls. It was obvious the owner had put a lot of thought and effort into creating a pleasant and inviting atmosphere.

I spent my days exploring the city and my nights unwinding in my cozy room, relishing the serenity and tranquility of the guesthouse.

The location was ideal, with the city's main attractions just a short walk away and the staff were cordial and helpful, always willing to provide recommendations and aid.

All in all, my experience at the guesthouse was fantastic, and I felt rejuvenated after my stay. I would highly recommend the guesthouse to other travelers, and I would consider staying there again if I had the chance to visit the city in the future.

In addition to traditional hotel and apartment options, Qatar also offers a number of unique accommodation options. For example, there are several desert camps that offer visitors the chance to experience the country's desert landscape and traditional Bedouin culture.

These camps typically include traditional tents or cabins, as well as activities such as camel rides and desert safaris.

Another unique accommodation option in Qatar is the opportunity to stay in a traditional Qatari house, known as a "qatari diar." These houses are typically made of coral and feature traditional Qatari architecture and decor. Staying in a qatari diar offers visitors the chance to experience traditional Qatari culture and hospitality firsthand.

Furthermore, many people prefer to stay in an area known as The Pearl, which is a man-made island located in the West Bay of Doha.

It is a luxurious area where most of the accommodation options are serviced apartments and villas. It's also known for its high-end shops, restaurants, and beach clubs.

Overall, Qatar offers a wide range of accommodation options to suit the needs and preferences of travelers, from luxury hotels to budget-friendly options and unique cultural experiences.

Chapter Six

What To Wear In Qatar

When visiting Qatar, it's important to dress modestly and respect the country's cultural and religious customs. For men, this means wearing long pants and a collared shirt, and for women, it means covering the shoulders and knees.

It's also recommended to avoid clothing with offensive graphics or writing. Additionally, it is best to avoid shorts and miniskirts, especially when visiting mosques or other religious sites. It's also important to note that Qatar can be quite hot, so lightweight, breathable fabrics are a good choice.

In addition to covering the shoulders and knees, it's also important for women to wear clothing that is not too tight-fitting, revealing, or transparent. Headscarves are not generally required for non-Muslims, but it is respectful to have the head covered, especially when visiting religious sites. It's also worth noting that during the month of Ramadan, it is expected for everyone to dress even more modestly and avoid eating, drinking, and smoking in public during the day.

In general, it's always a good idea to err on the side of caution when it comes to clothing in Qatar and to be respectful of the local customs and culture.

This will show that you are aware of and respectful of the local culture, and it will make your visit much more pleasant.

In respect to the climate in Qatar, it's advisable to wear lightweight, breathable fabrics such as cotton, linen, or rayon. These fabrics will help keep you cool in the hot and humid weather. It's also a good idea to dress in layers, so you can easily remove clothing if you get too warm. Long sleeves and pants will also help protect your skin from the sun.

In addition to covering the shoulders and knees, it's also important for women to wear clothing that is not too tight-fitting, revealing, or transparent.

Headscarves are not generally required for non-Muslims, but it is respectful to have the head covered, especially when visiting religious sites. You also should consider wearing sunglasses, a wide-brimmed hat and sunscreen with a high SPF rating to protect yourself from the sun.

Overall, it's best to dress modestly while also taking into consideration the hot and humid climate in Qatar. Light-colored and breathable clothing is recommended.

Chapter Seven

Food And Drinks You Will Find In Qatar

Qatar is known for its Middle Eastern cuisine, which features a mix of flavors and influences from the surrounding regions. Some popular foods and drinks found in Qatar include:

Machboos: a traditional dish made with rice, meat (usually chicken or lamb), and a variety of spices.

Shawarma: a Middle Eastern sandwich made with grilled meat (usually chicken or beef), tomatoes, lettuce, and various sauces wrapped in a pita bread.

Harees: a porridge-like dish made from wheat and meat (usually chicken or lamb).

Stuffed grape leaves: a traditional dish made by filling grape leaves with a mixture of rice, meat, and spices.

Falafel: a deep-fried ball or patty made from ground chickpeas or fava beans, often served in a pita bread with various toppings and sauces.

Qatari sweets: a variety of sweet treats such as balaleet (vermicelli pudding) and luqaimat (dumplings) are popular in Qatar.

Qatari coffee: a traditional coffee made with cardamom and served in small cups.

Dates: Qatar is known for its high-quality dates, which are often used in traditional dishes and as a sweet snack.

Camel milk: camel milk is popular in Qatar and is often consumed as a beverage or used in traditional dishes.

Qatari tea: a traditional tea made with mint leaves and served in small cups.

I have a clear recollection of my dining experience in Qatar. I traveled to a small town in the countryside and came across a restaurant that was renowned for its scrumptious food.

I made a reservation and arrived at the restaurant as the sun was setting, feeling eager to taste authentic Qatar cuisine. The atmosphere of the restaurant was cozy and inviting, with pictures of famous Qatar landmarks adorning the walls and candles on the tables creating a warm glow.

The host greeted me warmly and showed me to my table with a view of the garden. I had a hard time choosing from the many mouth-watering options on the menu.

Eventually, I went with the Machboos, a traditional dish made with rice, meat, and spices. I also ordered a bottle of red wine from the region and sat back to relish the ambiance of the restaurant while I waited for my meal.

When it arrived, I was amazed by the presentation and the delectable aroma. Every bite of my dinner was savored and I felt grateful for the chance to enjoy such delicious and authentic cuisine. The service at the restaurant was flawless and friendly.

Chapter Eight

Things To Do When You Spend Time In Qatar

Qatar is a country with a rich and diverse culture, and there are many things to see and do when you spend time there. Here are some suggestions for things to do when you visit Qatar:

Visit the Museum of Islamic Art in Doha: The Museum of Islamic Art (MIA) in Doha, Qatar is a world-class institution that showcases Islamic art and artifacts from across the globe. The museum's collection includes ceramics, metalwork, textiles, jewelry, and manuscripts from the 7th to the

19th century. The MIA building, designed by world-renowned architect I.M. Pei, is also a work of art in itself, featuring traditional Islamic architectural elements and modern design. The museum is open to the public from Saturday to Thursday, from 10:00 am to 5:00 pm, and on Fridays from 4:00 pm to 9:00 pm.

Explore the souqs (markets) in the historic district of Al Wakrah: However, I can tell you that the souqs (markets) in the historic district of Al Wakrah are a great place to experience traditional Qatari culture and shop for souvenirs such as traditional textiles, spices, and handicrafts. It's also a good place to get a sense of daily life in Qatar, as many locals shop at these markets for everyday goods.

The historic district of Al Wakrah is also known for its traditional architecture, which is worth exploring if you have the opportunity.

Take a desert safari to see the sand dunes and traditional Bedouin life.

Visit the Sheikh Faisal bin Qassim Al Thani Museum, which has a large collection of Islamic and Qatari artifacts.

Go shopping at the Villaggio Mall, which features a Venetian-style design and gondola rides.

Visit the Aspire Tower, which offers panoramic views of the city.

Visit the Katara Cultural Village, which has a variety of cultural and artistic events and exhibitions.

Go to the Pearl-Qatar, an artificial island with luxury shops, restaurants, and waterfront.

Watch a traditional Qatari dhow boat race at the Qatar Marine Sports Federation.

Visit the Al Thakira Mangroves, a protected area where you can spot different species of birds and marine life.

Chapter Nine

Health And Safety Tips

When traveling to Qatar, it is important to take precautions to maintain your health and safety. Here are a few tips to keep in mind:

- Make sure you are up-to-date on all required vaccinations, including those for measles, mumps, rubella, and polio.

- Drink only bottled water and avoid tap water and ice.

- Practice safe food handling and preparation, including washing your hands frequently and avoiding undercooked or raw foods.

- Take precautions to protect yourself from the sun, such as wearing sunscreen and protective clothing.

- Be aware of the risk of heat stroke, especially during the summer months.

- Understand the local laws and customs, including those related to dress and behavior.

- Be aware of the risk of terrorism and stay informed about potential threats.

- It is important to be aware that drug offenses are punishable by death in Qatar.

- Be aware that Qatar has strict laws regarding alcohol and its possession, so be careful with drinking.

It's always best to check for the latest travel advice from the government or embassy before you travel.